To Emz...

The New World Thought Disorder

ISBN: 978-0-244-85550-5

© 2020 The New World Thought Disorder

Lulu Press

London

The

New

World

Thought

Disorder

www.lulu.com/thenewworldthoughtdisorder

www.curioos.com/thenewworldthoughtdisorder

www.facebook.com/thenewworldthoughtdisorder

www.instagram.com/the_new_world_thought_disorder

www.twitter.com/TheNewWorldTho1

New

World

Thought

Disorder

Alan Peter Garfoot *Jnr. Cert. H.E. Dip.*

To My Sister Donna & Her Husband Steve

Immortalised On Your Wedding Day:

"In Sacred Rhyme,
May Your Love Shine,
For All Time"

Books & Publications:

www.lulu.com/spotlight/alangarfoot

Artwork:

www.artflakes.com/en/shop/newworldthoughtdisorder
www.curioos.com/newworldthoughtdisorder
www.saatchiart.com/account/profile/857306

Clothing:

www.shopvida.com/collections/voices/alan-a-p-garfoot
www.shop.spreadshirt.co.uk/newworldthoughtdisorder
www.cafepress.co.uk/newworldthoughtdisorder

Merchandise:

www.redbubble.com/people/alangarfoot
www.society6.com/alangarfoot

Facebook:

www.facebook.com/newworldthoughtdisorder

Contact E-Mail:

NewWorldThoughtDisorder@GMail.com

"A species which lives on only one planet,
Orbiting around only one star,
Considering the scale of the universe,
Is an endangered species."

'A.p.' (21/6/2012)

New World Thought Disorder

A book by: Alan Peter Garfoot

ISBN: 978-0-244-61473-7

Published In London:

By Lulu Press

New World Thought Disorder

Contents:

The Ideology of Greed

The famine enforcing capitalism,
Our enslavement to exploitative greed,
We sow the seeds of our destruction,
As millions starve and choke and bleed.

A selfish decadence blots our vision,
Children crying at night alone,
Global dominance the Western mission,
War-torn families forced from homes.

What of love and hope and beauty?
The ideals and values close to our hearts,
What are we creating for our future?
Burning all bridges here at the start.

Down with a system of decaying virtue,
Dead refugees by the thousands fleeing war,
Just images in the media that cannot hurt you,
When you glorify the rich you villainies the poor.

Guardians Of The World

Empower today; and tomorrow at dawn,
Feel our emotional steel tempered to form,
For within your love and compassion my kin,
The aspirational fire to inspire and a future to begin.

Those you adore; will be forevermore,
With a passion so great and a heart so pure,
For inside your heart I see treasure to behold,
Through your energy nexus you feel soul to soul.

Then in time infinite; your day will forever day be,
Upon the zenith of tomorrow you are forever free,
For with the orbs of destiny I see empathetic perfection,
Every potential manifesting through your affection.

So live true to yourself; and discover the beauty of your soul,
And flourish and thrive forever as guardians of the world...

Consensus of Corruption

A corporate consensus dominates,
Of elitist corruption and greed and hate,
A decay which binds to your will to create,
Till you cease to function through fatal mistakes.

The asphyxiation and panic as the toxin kicks in,
Of a soul in suffocation submerging in sin,
Drowning in dynamics where it's impossible to win,
Of the dark consecration which they now begin.

The media mind control of the masses through persuasion,
Consuming their superficial ideology of invasion,
Alienated to the truth through the mind control equation,
The media reinforcement of a politics of tactical evasion.

Enslavement to a system of competitive greed,
Based on their profit and not on social needs,
Decent of an asteroid poisoning a third of the seas,
The endangered human race & its iridium poisoned seeds.

The Mind-Control Equation

Ignorance,
The essence,
Of Alienated existence.
Virtue Distorted,
So as to represent,
A false image,
Of real true self.
So as to form,
An inwards dagger,
Of negative introspection.
A descending spiral,
Into an abyss of chaos.
To a penultimate situation,
Where we have no control,
And we can only lose.

Perfect Creation

Oh my sweetest beauty of the affection,
How I do desire your unique perfection,
Awake at night dreaming of you in my arms,
Delicate and protected safe from all harm.

The sublime grace of our souls attraction,
Alchemy of the heart in sacred reaction,
Our emotional dynamics entwined as one being,
Our spiritual essence connected through dreams.

<u>Cosmosis</u>

As I stretch out my mind,
Through the conscious essence,
Of our shared daydreams,
I open my inner vision,
To the glorious colours,
Of your heart and soul,
And together we drift,
Like fireflies dancing,
Upon a starlight breeze,
Our creative spontaneity,
Of infinite individuality,
For love is the essence,
As our stars collide.

Broken Perfection

Nymphea of perfected grace in elegant dance,
In your game of seduction I am so entranced,
An intellectual deduction of emotional circumstance,
An empathic connection to the gifted Hierophants.

The dynamic of your passion is an allure of the soul,
The pieces of your heart together we knit whole,
Your kindred essence of inspirational gold,
To free you through love is my passionate goal.

A being of beauty and of the purest of love,
Creating down below as resonates so above,
A sacred line of magic of ancient noble blood,
A being of a luscious elegance aligned to the good.

Virtue of vixen so gentle of form,
Heartbeat echoes of a person I adore,
A loving beauty inviting and warm,
To heal me anew when broken and torn.

Omnipathic

Essence of the immortal inner cosmos within ourselves,
Of the collective will of the universe evolving into itself.
The cosmic arts of the unifying interstellar vibration,
Are known through introspection upon the inner self,
For the revelation of the nature of what is truly real,
Must stir such a fascination and wonder within the soul.
A feeling of such raw power and incorruptible totality,
That one is created who can resist negative coercion,
For their truth is the passion within their hearts,
For the laws and facts of reason constitute my mind,
And through the synthesis of creative spontaneity,
The path to true joy and love to be found in the liberty,
Is known to the knave of the 'Great Chain of Being' as a youth,
But ideology is but the sad game of martyrs and fools,
And the Gods' do not shine down brightly on such ignorance,
But knowledge is the product of our capacity to understand,
And our true wisdom is our knowing when to act or intervene,
So our success is but the merit of luck in our positive endeavour,
Evolving our skills and capacities through which we can succeed,
So as that a being of pure and true essence and good intention,
As a totality of a will which echoes the oneness of the universe,
The duality of the unity of nature becomes a harmonic convergence,
And together within this undone space our enlightenment now begins.

All You've Ever Known

I've had some issues but haven't we all,
Sometimes we rise sometimes we fall,
With your love and hope I can stand tall,
All it takes is a text message e-mail or call.

Words can cut us to the bone,
But what are words when you've got no home,
When you walk the streets at night alone,
And a life of love is all you've known.

Focus upon these worded lines,
Feel the passion in these rhymes,
Know I am with you for all time,
For we are of the same design.

You need never cry or hide,
Know I am forever by your side,
With your strength, courage and hope and pride,
I know you will overcome all in your stride.

<u>Dedication</u>

To you my old companion I owe you this,
My effort and dedication in this life,
My focused drive and ethic of inspiration,
These things flowed to me from you,
Within the essence of my eternal soul,
I still feel your heartbeat inside,
So I quest onwards and upwards,
Always extending my horizons,
Through the vision of those around me,
So that a greater picture for us all,
Through our will shall come to manifest.

Kindred Spirit of Cosmic Emergence

Take root my kindred spirit of nature,
And grow in the fertile soil of your youth,
Grow and flourish as an eternal being,
Emerge in nature as one amongst equals,
All being unified in their uniqueness as individuals,
To create a new collective destiny for ourselves,
And explore our ability to redefine who we are,
Through the self-transcendent collective empathy,
Of the essence of the ideal of progressive freedom,
And achieve for ourselves oneness through individuality,
A shared ideology of empathy between all people,
And an equality through the liberation and freedom
Of a cultural synthesis aligned to the purest ideals,
So that as the brothers and sisters of Humanity,
Can all become people of planetary consciousness,
Together unique in the vast heavens of the stars.
Ready at last as an enlightened species of Earth,
To step out into the vast cosmos of the Universe.

The Immortal Soul

Beyond the standard representation of sensation,
Just outside the limits of the threshold of perception,
There exist realms of dimensions thought unknown,
Of a subtle gentle inner nature we nurture and grow,
Its achievement transcends everything we knew before,
So that way only the rarest originality knocks at their door,
And the purest compassion allows a unity of perspective,
Of those truly enlightened beings who are introspective,
Who listen for the pattern of the soul in our heartbeat,
In the vibration of the persons will and cognition,
To the dynamic of the fate within their life mission,
To hear for the voice of their destiny reborn in their name,
To feel the sacred echoes of our inner nature again,
Sealed within the essence of higher self we can find,
The eternal energy within a flux of between reality and mind,
So few will ever uncover their secrets of their alignment,
Of the inner introspective wisdom of our natures refinement,
We share in the uniting of the fragments of our being,
The golden empowerment of the immortality of dreams,
That truly comprehending the essence of the ego's order,
Within the emotional chaos of the nature of a destroyer,
That shard of divine light we have and of a freedom we feel within,
Through that unique human bond of love transcending immortal sin.

.

An Illuminating Path

Ancient creeds and paths entwining upon tangents,
The rapture of the eternal of cosmic soul and spirit,
The truest leaders of our entire collective existence,
Are of a shared universal cosmic enlightened essence,
So that those of all such levels of wisdom all share,
The universal vibration of a unifying consciousness,
A the dimensional energy of the spiritual mind-light,
We can heal and empower our once fragile broken beings,
Then inner self can manifest through refining our nature,
So that now through the key of the infinite of spirit,
We can access through our introspective focus,
The dynamics of the inner soul into emancipation,
The true joy and the pure satisfaction,
Of the realisation of our unique individuality,
In the potential of our higher nature as a species,
To evolve through abstract synthesis cultural perfection,
And a new narrative of positive progressive change.
So as that the Cosmic Human Race will emerge as Humanity,
Through respect, love and compassionate grace.

A Purple Rose of Individuality

Elegant strands he stroked her hair across her cheek,
The soft warmth of her face across the side of his hand,
Windswept with rapture and the rare awe of godhood,
They gently uncoiled into each other's arms,
The moment was truly the essence of the lovers.
Emotive intention focused beyond mere thoughts,
Lore of the inner will of meditative form and focus,
A peaceful clarity in our era the most sought,
For in chaos the mind is annihilated of useful ideas,
Lost in the whirlpool of the emotional essence,
Of the duality of your tangent caught in another's,
The progressive cascades of adoration between us,
Are the purest part of the potential of human nature,
Inspired through the agency of liberated freedom and hope,
The purple rose of a flourishing intellectual ideology
Of the social progression and unique spiritual emancipation,
Of a realisation of the legacy of the ideal of Humanity.

<u>Crystal Eyed Beauty</u>

Your beauty is so pure and unique,
Truly you are a cosmic princess,
Goddess of every exotic art,
Of a truly sublime subtle rapture,
The unique colour of your golden heart,
Every tone of the glory of true passion,
Subtle creature you are gorgeous,
As you lick your lips with hungry nature,
My the nature of my appetite grows,
Such a Diva of seduction and desire,
Of truly delicious affection you are,
Love struck I am captivated in awe,
By the essence of such angelic beauty,
Such grace and finesse of form,
True beauty of the soul you are to me,
Like the uniqueness of the cosmos itself.

Fractured Soul

Looking through the black mirror,
I gaze into an infinite abyss.
As I look deep into the void,
Shattered fragments,
Are all that remains,
Of a self,
A time,
Which once was.

Our Humanities Fate

Of the battle of this war and its final end,
For ideology is a mindless sacrificer,
Of a generation to the Gods of slaughter,
Are we not of such a human resemblance?
That we could put aside conflict and war?
That a positive progressive cause can be created?
How could unity between humanity be found?
And war and cultural conflict meet its end?
Of what is highest and truest victory or battle?
But the one where war be ended eternally.
But what hope truly is there for the human race?
To stop the ruthless cultural self-infatuation,
With the egotism of profit, power, conquest and war?
Fuelling the corruption of unaccountable leaders,
Blood on our hands for diamonds, opium and oil,
Stripping our sacred planet bare and barren,
Of her minerals and resources,
What victory is there to be had?
Against the essence of this decay of the soul?
Of the flourishing of the positive potential of humanity,
Versus a cancerous conquest of cosmic tragedy,
The empowerment of an oppressive Human Race?
To an interstellar legacy of mindless totalitarian consumption?
I hope not...

To The Stars...

Delicate beauty of heavens secret arts,
Across the void I feel the beat of your heart,
With a tender essence so loving in soul,
I desire to make your circle whole.

When ancient lines of noble blood converge,
The essence of perfection in you will emerge.
Lovers of wisdom introspect to your soul,
Then emotional will shall be yours to control.

Creative creature set your wild spirit free,
Communicate with stars and share your energy with trees.
Inspire all you meet with the concepts of creation,
To align the world soul to our passions inspiration.

Let us fly through our dreams to planets off far,
Pursuing our hearts as we travel star to star.
So awaken the spiritual code embedded in your genes,
And discover what it means to become an enlightened being.

Midsummer Rain

Heat of the baking midday sun,
Spreading the strength of summertime,
As a thunderstorm beckons overhead,
The rain pours on down,
But doesn't dampen our spirits,
Forever free in the garden of youth,
Lightning flickers across the skies,
Setting our hearts alive,
The thunderbolt echo's around,
And from within the tension is released,
Freedom truly in the summer of love,
The love of those teenage days,
Essence of youth our passions,
Of sacred aspiration and inspirations,
We roam free as kings and queens,
Our friendship welded by our uniqueness,
That with each other we have found,
True individuality and uniqueness,
That between us freedom shall forever reign.

Objective Epiphany

Do you accept a truth?
Which will weaken you,
And leave you vulnerable.

Or believe a lie?
Which will make you stronger,
So you can survive.

Fairies Of The Twilight Moon

Upon wings of the essence of the air,
Transformed evolved beings enlightened,
We take flight to the night together,
Sailing on warm currents of spirit,
In the midnight moons soft glow,
Like moths to the flame we dance,
We sail upwards into the skies twilight frost,
Our bodies frozen still we glide then fall,
As we descend warmth returns to true wings,
Inspiration forms and aspiration returns,
And we rise once more to the occasion,
Of the moons sacred crystalline radiance,
As the butterfly fairies of the twilight stars,
In the Lords of nature's celestial dance.

Spark of Life

If God is infinite,
Then all of creation,
As the infinity within,
Of the divine soul,
The higher self I feel,
Our connection to nature,
And the cosmos above,
We can comprehend,
As a spark of light inside,
Within the subconscious mind,
For what is without limit,
In essence is everything,
That has; is and will ever occur,
So as part of our divine right,
To develop this connection,
And emerge as true individuals,
Of planetary awareness and unity,
An interstellar enlightenment,
So that we too can become gods,
Refining the resonance of our will,
To the essence of perfection,
A reflection of infinity.

Mode of Production

All should have access to study or learn a trade,
So then we can aspire to a higher than minimum wage,
A qualification that you can study for free at any age,
Because at the end of the day we all want to get paid.

Made to work for benefits as a corporations slave,
The consumption of destruction every single day,
Persecution of the poor the rightwing political craze,
The corruption of social function by capitalisms ways.

So take to the streets with industrial action,
Protest your rights against benefit sanctions,
Overcome the satisfaction of consumerist distraction,
Blind to the reality of the social reaction.

<u>Thought Revolution</u>

Thought is a product of intuition,
Designed for a cosmic mission,
To inspire you through creative vision,
The virtue to make your own decisions.

Project unto the astral plains,
Program skills into our brains,
Overcome the spiritual pain,
And try not to go insane.

Through words and rhythm try to inspire,
A spiritual path of enlightened desire,
Where we all try to aim higher,
To empower those who hope and aspire.

So conquer the chaos of confusion,
Dissolve away sadness and delusion,
Seek inside your own solutions,
And join the new world thought revolution.

Consensus of Corruption

As long as the rich abuse the poor,
I see nothing but suffering and perpetual war,
Because Trump like every tyrant who came before,
Will deviate and then break international law,
Then we go into the Middle East for another tour,
With another landing on foreign shores,
With antiterrorism as our noble cause,
Repeated and repeated to the point where it bores,
So what are these invasions actually for?
Well our oil reserves have limits that's for sure,
And the ideology of our hypocrisy rots to the core,
When the use of chemical weapons in Syria we all saw,
The untold horrors of a country war-torn,
But did we not stop or think to pause,
Now ISIS and Fascist's are at our door,
That we have no clue for what is now in store,
But doesn't it make you feel sore and so raw,
That instead of research into a solution global energy cure,
We follow lies that only we, our God or race is pure,
Brainwashed so much extreme beliefs become yours.

Lovely Cosmos

Oh my sweet beauty of the stars,
Your soft tender nature,
I do so adore.
For your heart,
My own beats true,
Such love and passion,
From deep within the soul,
Your essence is such divine energy,
With your cosmic aura,
You empower and inspire,
A sense of feeling,
Deep within my core.
From the meaning of my meanings,
The thought of my thoughts,
A higher consciousness descends,
And deeper self-awareness develops,
The creation of an inspired cosmic love,
Essence of our highest nature.

Illegitimate Culture

Do not war my brothers and sisters,
For you are still kindred spirits,
And we all share our one planet Earth,
Can we not empathise and see each other,
Through each other's eyes and understand,
The brethren bond of humanity,
As a part of our enlightened human nature,
The concepts of our cognition aligned,
Energised by the will of pure intention,
Into our fundamental state of mind,
Which all of humanity shares together?
Are we not of a likeness enough?
That we can put aside our differences,
And express the emergence of our humanity,
To care for and nurture our new growth,
That one day we will all shine with freedom,
From the end of the culture of war and violence,
As a legitimate culture of human interaction.

First Frost of the Dawn

The truest of the enlightened of heart,
Masters of the light of the heavens,
From which the arts of true inspiration flow,
As like a song of the purest love.
In the essence of their aura and energies,
You feel the resonance of their pure soul,
And the dynamics of the passion they share,
For from deep within their core,
The profound grace of their love manifests,
Their flourishing love knowing no limits,
Such is the glory of their emancipated being,
A luscious golden light surrounds,
The perfection of their true destiny,
Lying right within their grasp,
Such are the stars aligned for them,
That they share the moon at night,
And together share the warm sunshine,
Sailing upon the morning dawn rays.

Summer Sun

Heat of the summer sun,
Its light warming us gently,
Permeating all of our beings,
We share in its golden glory,
Sweet scent of the flowers,
Nectar of the pollen filling my lungs,
The essence of the midsummer perfume,
Hanging delicately in the air,
With your arms around me,
Such closeness is so rare,
In a world of cold indifference,
Truly I feel so complete,
A heart so pure and perfect,
Deep I am fascinated by your being,
Such a capacity of true originality,
That most unique characteristic,
Most perfected quality of your heart,
I feel in the mid-day heat,
Of the resplendent summer sun.

Immortal of the Stars

That familiar presence lovers feel,
A warm essence of such uniqueness,
That they feel all around themselves.
That across the distance between them,
Separating dreams and stars,
There is a another being like them,
Whose heart dreams deep and wide?
Of a gentle love and soft passion,
A purity of love so true and rare,
Spiritual in kind yet bold and free,
Who yearns for another like themselves?
A vision of love to walk out of their dreams,
To hold the water cold or hot,
Of the true emotion in their ideals,
And be with them together forevermore,
Their lover of life and compassionate other,
Unique of aspiration and equal of inspiration,
Throughout all of the manifest universe,
An immortal of truest eternal love.

True To Life

Stand tall and true to form,
Realise the queen within the pawn,
And break the silence upon the dawn,
As our fallen are re-born.

Give to others the gift of hope,
And tie your knot in Awen's rope,
So that through empathy we can cope,
For humanity is within our races scope.

So remember of heart to try and be kind,
And try to be part open of mind,
For our fate is not set but part our design,
Determined by the pieces we have refined.

Kindred Footsteps

A wish projected unto the heavens,
With the hope of manifest magnificence,
Ambitions of a heart still wild in nature,
Dreams of the ideal are conjured forth,
Desires of a heart touched by heaven arise,
Questing for what is good and pure,
Upon a path of the truest of visions,
Mission unto the lord of all lords,
Dedication inside to the truest love,
Strength be mine in times of strife,
And endurance be mine in adverse times,
May the heart take root and grow in my soul,
And hopes and aspirations become,
In the actualisation of what I feel inside,
For success is just beyond the horizon,
In the achievement of order out of chaos,
And the recognition of my endeavours by my kin.

<u>Shooting Star</u>

Oh my shooting star,
How I admire you so,
Purity & clarity of your heart,
Lushness of your divine nature,
And passion of your immortal soul,
Inspire these mere humble words,
But pale and faded reflections,
Of the perfected essence of your love,
Your golden empowering light,
Surrounding and pervading my being,
Burning away the shadows of sorrow,
Uplifting my spirit through gentle grace,
Replenished and transformed through love,
With the influence of guardian angels,
So as that our love will always be strong,
As like a light high up in the heavens,
Burning bright in the sky for all time,
As like true immortals of the cosmos.

Limelight First Sight

Deep inside I lock on the flow,
Mood is set I feel the groove,
Timing perfect soft and slow,
Velvet soft and silky smooth.

In the bass I feel the rhythm,
As manifests the tribal vibe,
Spontaneous look make quick decisions,
For fools do not feel from inside.

Searching for the truest meanings,
Feeling tired and feeling worn,
Trying to create a positive feeling,
Someplace happy and somewhere warm.

Temper your actions out of desire,
For you have the right to know,
Stare with me into this fire,
Then past and future I can show.

8 Years On...

Eight years since I last looked into your eyes,
Yet every day you still light up my skies.

It's been so many years since you have gone,
But still close to my heart it doesn't seem so long.

Today you would have been sixty seven,
But instead today you're looking down from heaven,

You were a father, a friend, a role model and gaffer,
Every day you filled my heart with so much laughter,

The Guinness and the jokes like my stealthy foul socks,
Dad you were my hero and man you fucking rocked,

Turning on the hot tap when I was in the shower,
Then up for a meeting with clocks forwards four hours,

Fishing on the Ancholme soaking up the rays,
Living with you Dad were the best of my days,

I still hear your voice like a Druid with the birds,
And I immortalise your life with my written words,

You had the brains, the brawn, the heart and looks,
And now your name on twenty five books.

Bleak Life on Streets

What do you do when you have lost your home?
When you walk the streets at night alone,
When the cold wind cuts you to the bone,
When a life of hardship is all you've known.

Cut out of the system by benefit sanctions,
While the world is consumed by consumerist distractions,
Safe from all harm by superficial satisfactions,
When it's about time somebody took some action.

It's hard to imagine a life so bleak,
As a person who is forced to live on the streets,
With so many excluded how can society be complete,
When our freedom of speech is only freedom to compete.

With more people laid off through downsizing corporations,
No employment or career guaranteed by the nation,
So is it any surprise that after a decade of hesitation,
Thousands take to the streets in political demonstration.

www.ingramcontent.com/pod-product-compliance
Lightning Source LLC
Chambersburg PA
CBHW030306030426
42337CB00012B/607